HEINEMANN
Profiles

S e a n   C o n n o l l y

Heinemann

Sch

D1424229

First published in Great Britain by Heinemann Library, Halley Court, Jordan Hill, Oxford OX2 8EJ, a division of Reed Educational and Professional Publishing Ltd. Heinemann is a registered trademark of Reed Educational & Professional Publishing Limited.

OXFORD MELBOURNE AUCKLAND JOHANNESBURG BLANTYRE GABORONE IBADAN PORTSMOUTH NH (USA) CHICAGO

Designed by Visual Image
Originated by Dot Gradations
Printed and bound in Hong Kong/China

05 04 03 02 01
10 9 8 7 6 5 4 3 2 1

ISBN 0 431 08636 2
This title is also available in a hardback library edition (ISBN 0 431 08629 X)

British Library Cataloguing in Publication Data

Connolly, Sean
Nelson Mandela. – (Heinemann Profiles)
1. Mandela, Nelson, 1918- – Juvenile literature 2. Presidents – South Africa – Biography – Juvenile lierature
3. Anti-apartheid movements – South Africa – History – Juvenile literature
I. Title
968'.06'092
ISBN 0431086362

Acknowledgements
The Publishers would like to thank the following for permission to reproduce photographs:
Associated Press: p30, J-M Bouju p47; Bailey's African History Archives: pp22, 27, Drum pp14, 16, 26, A Kumalo p31, Peter Magubane pp4, 28, Jurgen Schadeberg pp20, 24; Penni Bickle: p33; Corbis-Bettmann/UPI: p8; Mayibuye Centre: pp7, 13, 19, 34; Popperfoto: Reuters p39; Rex Features: pp10, 25, 29, 40, 42, 44, 45, 46, 48, 49, 50, Nils Jorgensen p37, M Zeffler p43.

Cover photograph reproduced with permission of Rex Features

Every effort has been made to contact copyright holders of any material reproduced in this book. Any omissions will be rectified in subsequent printings if notice is given to the Publisher.

For more information about Heinemann Library books, or to order, please phone ++44 (0)1865 888066, or send a fax to ++44 (0)1865 314091. You can visit our website at www.heinemann.co.uk.

Any words appearing in the text in bold, **like this**, are explained in the Glossary.

CONTENTS

WHO IS NELSON MANDELA?

Nelson Mandela has always faced the future with optimism and confidence.

A s the twentieth century drew to a close, people looked back at the last hundred years to try to make sense of all the changes that had taken place. There had been two terrible world wars, in which millions of people died, as well as further wars and conflicts that look set to continue into the new millennium. For some observers, it seems as though there is no way in which hatred and injustice can be defeated.

SHINING EXAMPLE

Other people take a more hopeful view, looking at the work of brave individuals who have suffered greatly in order to promote peace and equality. Nelson Mandela is one such individual. Born in a country in which the **majority** of the population was denied basic human rights, he nevertheless managed to educate himself and become a leading figure in the efforts to improve life in South Africa. In the end, he did succeed in improving life in his country.

Along the way, Nelson suffered even more than his countrymen from the harsh system in South Africa. The cruel system of **apartheid** made it almost impossible to find good housing, work or even the means to travel within his own country. In addition to this, his efforts to promote change led to nearly 30 years in prison.

EXTENDING A HAND

Nelson Mandela's long period in prison only strengthened his will to improve life in his country. The world gradually became aware of his aims and offered support to his cause. Nelson Mandela waited patiently until a South African leader arrived who was prepared to heed this support, and who was willing to release Mandela from prison.

Without sacrificing any of his ideals, Nelson Mandela emerged from prison and was able almost immediately to change the face of South Africa. Again, the world welcomed his efforts. He never professed to be a saint – simply a man with an unswerving determination to make his country a proper home for all who live there. Even as leader of South Africa he met difficulties but he has led the country by his own example of courage, decency and fairness. For these simple virtues – tested by the harshest opposition – he remains an example for the whole world.

A RURAL CHILDHOOD

Nelson Mandela was born on 18 July 1918 in a tiny village called Mvezo in the region of South Africa known as Transkei. This area is rich farming country, with rolling hills, fertile soil and many rivers to keep the land well watered. Most people in Transkei lived – and still live today – in small villages like Mvezo. The most important person in such villages is the chief, a man who makes many decisions and often settles disputes between villagers.

A ROYAL CONNECTION

Nelson's father, Gadla Henry Mphakanyiswa Mandela, was the chief in Mvezo. He also had another important connection – with the royal family of the Thembu people who lived in that part of Transkei. Nelson's father, like his father before him, was trained to **counsel** the Thembu kings. Part of this role was to **chronicle** the history of the Thembu people, as well as the larger Xhosa nation of which they are a part.

It is common for Thembu chiefs to have more than one wife. Gadla Mphakanyiswa had four wives, and Nelson's mother was the chief's fourth wife, Nosekeni Fanny. Altogether the chief had four sons and nine daughters. The youngest boy, who grew to become the famous Nelson Mandela, was named Rolihlahla, which means 'pulling the branch of the tree' in the Xhosa language. He was given the name 'Nelson' by a teacher when he was a small boy. Admiral Horatio Nelson had been a famous British hero, and the teacher thought that a black child would get on better in life if the British rulers could recognize and pronounce his name.

Traditional Transkei houses were built to reflect the intense heat of the sun in South Africa.

Uprooted

The British ruled South Africa when Nelson was a child. They accepted some of the tribal divisions among black South Africans because the divisions made the country as a whole easier to rule. The Thembu were one of many such groupings of black South Africans. When Nelson was a baby his father, a proud man, had a disagreement with a local British **magistrate** and lost his position. Nelson and three of his sisters had to leave Mvezo with their

The great Indian leader, Mahatma Gandhi, trained as a lawyer in South Africa in order to fight injustice. Nelson's early career would take the same path.

mother and move to another village, Qunu, where Nelson spent most of his childhood. Nelson's mother had family there, and they were able to help support them. The family had little money but Nelson and the other village boys were free to play in the veld and to look after the villagers' sheep and cattle.

At home in the evening Nelson's mother would tell the children about the history and legends of the Xhosa people. These stories made a great impression on the young boy, who became very proud of his nation's history.

South Africa in the 1920s

South Africa was controlled by the British in the 1920s. The British had gained full control over South Africa after defeating **Afrikaners** in the Boer War, which ended in 1902. Britain united the different parts of South Africa in the Act of Union of 1910. At the same time it offered limited freedom of government to some of the parts of South Africa which were previously ruled by the Afrikaners. The Afrikaners, like the British, were white. The position for non-white South Africans – and in particular for black South Africans – was very different. In some parts of South Africa, a tiny **minority** of blacks and **coloureds** could vote, but real power lay with the white rulers. Black South Africans were able to look after some of their affairs locally, as in the Thembu Court of Justice (see page 11), but the black population had no real say in how the country itself was run.

A GLIMPSE OF POWER

When Nelson was nine years old his father came to Qunu to visit that branch of his large family. He was very tired and was suffering from a serious lung disease. After several days of rest in one of the family's huts, Nelson's father died. Nelson was very sad, but his mother had another problem as well as her own sadness – how to bring up her children without any income.

As a teenager, Nelson Mandela enjoyed many benefits of his family's royal connection.

THE ROYAL HOUSEHOLD

Nelson's family connection with the royal family of Thembuland came to the rescue. Chief Jongintaba Dalindyebo, the **regent** of the royal family, offered to act as Nelson's **guardian**. The chief considered him to be, in effect, part of his extended family. Nelson had to leave the village and his friends to move to the regent's home in Mqhekezweni, the capital of Thembuland. Nelson's mother went with him to the new home, but then had to return to her other children in Qunu after a few days.

Life in the new home was very different from anything Nelson had seen before. He saw motor cars and electric lights as well as far more white people. One of the regent's responsibilities was to settle disputes – much as Nelson's own father had done, but on a larger scale. In this role, the regent **presided** over the Thembu Court of Justice. Nelson would watch and listen as the court heard cases. These cases influenced Nelson greatly, and he was determined to become a lawyer. In the large house he also listened to the conversations of the **elders** of the Thembu people. They spoke of the many wars that their **ancestors** had fought in defence of their lands. These stories influenced Nelson, who began to consider the freedom struggle of his people.

A GOOD EDUCATION

The regent insisted that Nelson should have all of the advantages that his own children enjoyed. One of these was a good education, so Nelson was sent to Clarkebury Boarding Institute when he was sixteen years old. He studied hard at this school and made friends with the other young Thembu boys and girls there. In 1937, when he was nineteen, Nelson enrolled at Healdtown, which educated young Africans in much the same way as an English college. Very few black people had this opportunity, and Nelson benefited from the regent's wealth.

Nelson had a difficult timetable at Healdtown, although the discipline there would serve him well in later life. Students woke at six in the morning and began a long day's work, with only skimpy meals to break up the studies which would last until five. There would be more studying in the evening until lights went out at 9.30.

One day, near the end of Nelson's year at Healdtown, the students were addressed by a famous Xhosa poet, Krune Mqhayi. Nelson was startled to hear Mqhayi's words. Speaking in Xhosa, the poet made a powerful prediction – that one day, black Africans would rule themselves. The words were dramatic and Nelson took them as an order directed to himself.

LIFELONG FRIENDS

Obeying the regent's wishes, Nelson enrolled at the University College of Fort Hare in 1938. This establishment was the only place of higher learning for black Africans at that time. Nelson was **groomed** to become the first member of the regent's **clan** to obtain a university degree. Fort Hare had been founded as a **missionary** college, and it still insisted on Christian behaviour from its students. However, it was also a centre for proud young Africans to learn more about their own culture and history. Many of the teachers agreed with the words Nelson had heard from Mqhayi, and the students constantly debated the African struggle amongst themselves. Many of them hoped that the black **majority** would one day come to rule the country.

One of the friends Nelson made in these discussions was a serious science student named Oliver Tambo. This new friend was a good debater and he always listened to what the others said before opening his mouth. The two young men spent a lot of time together, attending church services as well as the lively student debates.

Nelson was also gaining a reputation as a quick thinker and good speaker. He was elected to the Student's Representative Council (SRC). This new position soon landed him in trouble. The SRC insisted on better food at Fort Hare and threatened a **boycott** if conditions did not improve. The authorities refused the demand and Nelson was **expelled** from Fort Hare.

Oliver Tambo was to become Nelson's life long friend and ally in South Africa's struggle for freedom.

LIFE IN THE CITY

Nelson was worried when he returned to Mqhekezweni. He knew that the **regent** would be furious when he learned how the young man's 'antics' had got him **expelled** from Fort Hare. The regent made his position clear – Nelson must be prepared to abandon the Fort Hare **boycott** and return the following year. Those were the conditions that the authorities at Fort Hare had offered when Nelson left.

Walter Sisulu convinced Nelson of the need to continue with his studies.

A FORCED HAND

Back at Mqhekezweni Nelson resumed his normal activities, helping the regent and watching as cases were tried. He was pleased when the regent's son, named Justice, joined him. The two young men had become close friends during Nelson's years at Mqhekezweni, and they looked forward to more good times. But then the pair of them had some upsetting news: the regent was planning a marriage for each of the young men. This was devastating since neither young man really knew the young woman that he was meant to marry. It also seemed to spell the end of their independence.

Both Nelson and Justice knew that the regent would not agree if the young men asked to remain unmarried for the time being. He was simply doing what was expected of him – making sure that the **clan** continued into the next generation. In 1940 Nelson and Justice decided that their only choice was to run away and start a new life.

THE BIG CITY

Nelson and Justice made their way by train to South Africa's largest city, Johannesburg. They had their passes (see page 17) but needed to get other documents, such as a letter from a boss, once they arrived in the big city. After some difficulties along the way they finally found themselves jobs at Crown Mines, the largest gold mine in Johannesburg. Within a day, though, the boys' new boss found out that they had run away and dismissed them.

Now they were alone in the big city with no jobs and no money. Nelson and Justice decided to try to find work separately and to meet again in the George Goch **township**, where a cousin of Nelson's lived. The cousin was impressed by Nelson's determination and helped him meet influential

people. One of these people was a successful young
businessman named Walter Sisulu. Nelson was
deeply affected by the sight of a fellow black man
who seemed confident in the world of
Johannesburg. Walter advised Nelson to continue his
education with the aim of becoming a lawyer. He
could do this by taking a **correspondence course**,
but in the meantime Nelson needed a job.

LEARNING THE LAW

Walter also found a job for Nelson, with the legal
firm of Witkin, Sidelsky and Eidelman. One of the
partners in this firm, Lazar Sidelsky, was a friend of
Walter's and was eager to promote the education
and training of young black lawyers. Sidelsky agreed
to take Nelson on as an **articled clerk**, providing
Nelson with an income and a chance to see law in
action. In the evenings Nelson studied by

correspondence with the University of South Africa in order to gain the degree that was also necessary to become a lawyer.

The law firm was an ideal place for Nelson to meet white people who were kind and who had no **prejudice** against black South Africans. By making friends with others who worked there he met people from the various **ethnic** backgrounds that make up South Africa – not just blacks and whites, but Indians and **coloureds**. At night, though, Nelson had to return to Alexandra, one of the townships where blacks lived. Alexandra lacked electricity and there was a great deal of crime, but most of the people did their best to help each other out.

Pass laws

For many years it was difficult for black South Africans to travel within their country. The government insisted that each black person, known as an 'African' as opposed to a white person, carry a special pass. This document was like a passport, except people needed to show them to white policemen inside their own country whenever they were asked. The pass acted as a way of controlling where black people lived and worked. A person faced arrest and even a prison sentence for failing to produce a pass.

JOINING THE MOVEMENT

Nelson was still working for the law firm in Johannesburg and studying at night when he learned in 1942 that the **regent** had died. Nelson and his former guardian had had several disagreements about Nelson's independent spirit, but the death of the older man saddened Nelson greatly. He returned to Mqhekezweni for the funeral and found he was teased for the way his Xhosa pronunciation had changed. In the relatively short time he had lived in Johannesburg Nelson had acquired a slight Zulu accent. Rather than feel ashamed by this, Nelson simply felt that the change in his speech reflected the way in which he now felt closer to all South Africans regardless of their background. Justice took on the role as the regent, but Nelson returned to the big city to pursue his own plans.

PART OF THE STRUGGLE

Later in 1942 Nelson passed the final examination for his **BA degree**. He also became more friendly with a fellow worker named Gaur, who spoke at length of the need for black Africans to improve their own conditions. He took Nelson along to meetings of the African National Congress (ANC), where Nelson saw passionate debates about subjects ranging from racial equality to bus fares.

After attending several meetings Nelson realised that Walter Sisulu was one of the leaders in the organization. Nelson began spending much of his free time at Walter's house in the Orlando district. Discussions continued long into the night, often accompanied by huge meals cooked by Walter's mother. Nelson became a member of the ANC and began to become well known in the local area for his intelligence and dedication. There were other familiar faces joining Nelson at these meetings. Among them was his old friend Oliver Tambo.

Nelson married trainee nurse Evelyn Mase after meeting her at Walter Sisulu's house.

ATTRACTING THE YOUNG

One of the ANC members that Nelson and Oliver met at Walter's house was a young lawyer named Anton Lembede. He was one of the few black lawyers in South Africa, so Nelson paid particular attention to what he said. Lembede was a forceful speaker and complained that the ANC was stuck in the past. In his view, the ANC leadership was too timid and approached the struggle for black independence in the wrong way. Instead of polite **petitions** to the white government, and acting strictly within the unfair rules set out by the government, he wanted the ANC to be more **aggressive**. The movement needed to show the government that it represented the vast **majority** of South Africans, and not just a core of well-educated black people in the cities.

Always well dressed, Nelson knew that he was an example for other young African leaders.

Nelson and Oliver Tambo agreed with Lembede's views about the ANC and the need for change. Like him, they wanted the struggle for freedom to be more of a **grassroots** movement, appealing to the uneducated as well as those living in the countryside. In particular, the ANC needed to attract younger members. With this aim in mind, Nelson Mandela, Oliver Tambo, Walter Sisulu and about 60 other ANC members set about forming a youth branch of the ANC. They worked within the organization to do this and on Easter Sunday 1944, in a social centre in Johannesburg, they officially launched the ANC Youth League (ANCYL).

The African National Congress

The African National Congress (ANC) was formed in 1912 as a way of improving the living conditions of the black majority in South Africa. It was the oldest national African organization in the country and it tried to attract members from the many tribal groups that make up South Africa. At the time of the ANC's **founding**, and for many years afterwards, blacks could not vote, own land or travel freely in their own country. The goal of the ANC was to make black people full citizens of South Africa. However, unlike groups with similar aims in other African countries, the ANC wanted the change to come from within the existing system. The ANC **constitution** banned **radical** activities and violence and concentrated on stating its aims with polite dignity.

A RISING STAR

N elson impressed his fellow ANC members with his discipline and determination. He was elected to the **Secretaryship** of the ANCYL in 1947. Along with Walter Sisulu, Oliver Tambo and other young ANC members, Nelson promoted the idea of change within the movement.

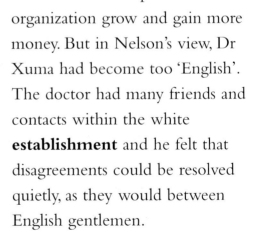

INTERNAL BATTLES

Not everyone was pleased with the changing attitude of young ANC members. In particular, Dr A B Xuma, head of the ANC, felt that things were changing too fast. Dr Xuma was well respected within the ANC because he had helped the organization grow and gain more money. But in Nelson's view, Dr Xuma had become too 'English'. The doctor had many friends and contacts within the white **establishment** and he felt that disagreements could be resolved quietly, as they would between English gentlemen.

This clash of ideas became more apparent after the general election of 1948. As in other South African elections, only whites could vote.

Afrikaner Nationalist Dr DF Malan addressing a large crowd of supporters.

The Programme of Action

The Programme of Action was one of many important documents that Nelson Mandela helped write for the ANC. It set specific goals for the ANC in its fight against injustice. The main demands were that all South Africans have equal rights as citizens, in education, **parliamentary representation**, property ownership and work. And unlike most previous ANC documents it presented its aims as a series of demands rather than requests. Nelson and other leading ANC members spoke at illegal meetings around the country, explaining the ANC position to fellow blacks and building **grassroots** support.

The new government, under the National Party, formed a harsh new system of laws known as **apartheid**. The previous system of mostly unofficial restrictions against blacks was bad enough, but the new apartheid laws made life even harder for the non-white **majority**. Young ANC members felt that they must be more forceful in their defiance of the new laws so they drew up a Programme of Action.

The programme, which Nelson, Oliver Tambo and Walter Sisulu helped draw up, called for the ANC to use the weapons of strikes, **boycotts** and **civil disobedience**. The programme became official ANC policy in 1949 when Dr JS Moroka replaced the **conservative** Dr Xuma as ANC president. Younger men began to replace older members throughout the ANC and in 1950 Nelson was elected to the National Executive Committee (NEC) of the ANC.

THE STRUGGLE CONTINUES

With its dynamic new leadership the ANC continued to press its case for equality within South Africa. In 1952 it launched its Campaign for the Defiance of Unjust Laws. Again, Nelson played an important role, this time as National Volunteer-in-Chief. This post meant Nelson travelled around South Africa persuading ordinary people to defy the harsh **apartheid** laws. For his part in this campaign Nelson and others in the campaign were arrested under the Suppression of Communism Act. The judge, whom Nelson respected, agreed that the men had not encouraged people to use violence, so they got only a **suspended sentence** of two years. This sentence meant, however, that Nelson was not allowed to attend gatherings or to leave Johannesburg.

LEGAL ACTION

Nelson put his time to good use and achieved all the qualifications to practise law. In 1952 Nelson and Oliver Tambo opened their own legal office in Johannesburg. The two lawyers tried to help their clients – most of whom were also non-whites – in their struggle against the apartheid laws. Nelson's knowledge of the law would help him in later years.

Nelson in the offices he shared with Oliver Tambo.

At the 1952 Annual Conference of the ANC Chief Albert Luthuli was elected president, replacing Dr Moroko. Nelson Mandela was appointed First Deputy President. Nelson took his responsibilities seriously and campaigned for better education and living conditions for all South Africans. At the same time he continued to practise law.

In late 1957 Nelson was charged again, this time with **treason**. He was among a number of ANC members who were singled out because of their prominence. The government argued that the ANC leadership had been preparing to overthrow the government by violence and to replace it with a **communist** government. The trial lasted a long time.

In June 1958 Nelson married his second wife, Winnie Nomzamo Madikizela. Nelson and his first wife Evelyn had divorced because she did not agree with Nelson's deep involvement with the ANC.

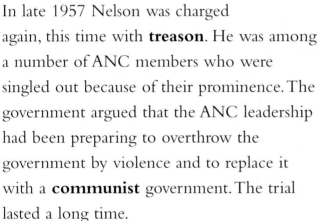

'We had risen in professional status in our community, but every case in court, every visit to the prisons to interview clients, reminded us of the humiliation and suffering burning into our people.'

Oliver Tambo, recalling his legal partnership with Nelson Mandela

AN UNFOLDING DRAMA

The late 1950s, when Nelson's **treason** trial was in progress, saw many changes in Africa. The European **colonial** powers, such as the UK and France, were granting independence to many former colonies.

SHARPEVILLE

At the same time, nothing was really changing in South Africa. The government was putting into practice its **Bantustan** policy, which forced many black South Africans to move into government-approved **homelands**. Nelson Mandela argued forcefully against this policy, and his actions led to several **banning orders**.

Nelson and his fellow defendants remained confident throughout their long treason trial.

By now black South Africans had mounted several large protests against **apartheid**. In March 1960 several thousand gathered in the **township** of Sharpeville near Johannesburg. The 75 police present panicked, opening fire on the unarmed demonstrators. Within seconds, 69 demonstrators lay dead. The reaction to this

The Sharpeville tragedy forced the ANC to continue their struggle by means of arms.

tragedy echoed around the world. The South African government responded by declaring a **State of Emergency** and by making the ANC illegal. From then on, the ANC had to continue its struggle **underground**.

BATTLE LINES

A rare piece of good news cheered the ANC on 29 March 1961, when the treason trial involving Nelson Mandela collapsed. Nelson took more part in the secret ANC plans and helped launch a new branch of the ANC. This new group, called Umkhonto we Sizwe (Spear of the Nation) but known to most people simply as MK, would be the armed core of the ANC and would prepare to continue the struggle by force. Nelson was to be its Chief. In effect, his task was to form an army. And although Nelson was technically free, after the collapse of the treason trial, he knew that the government was waiting to arrest him again. He felt that his only chance of continuing his job was to move secretly around the country, keeping one step ahead of those who would be on his trail.

Nelson represented the ANC at the All-in Africa conference in 1961.

Nelson was breaking many **apartheid** laws in his travels around the country and there was a **warrant** for his arrest issued almost as soon as he went on the run. The continued freedom of such a public figure, particularly someone as well known as Nelson Mandela, rubbed salt in the wounds of the police. With each day that passed they increased their efforts to trap Nelson.

THE BLACK PIMPERNEL

Nelson's main strategy was to find a hiding place where he could stay during the day, concentrating on his work during the night. The ANC and other organizations helped locate **safe houses** where Nelson could stay, sometimes for months at a time. The other way in which Nelson remained on the run was to become 'invisible'. He took less care with his appearance, knowing that the vast majority of black South Africans could not afford to look as smart as he normally did. One of Nelson's best disguises was as a **chauffeur** as he had the use of a car. People would think that he was on an errand for his white 'master'.

Nelson and Oliver Tambo meeting in Ethiopia in 1962.

Nelson also made daring reports to the newspapers, **taunting** the government in an effort to raise the spirit of the black **majority**. Nelson's exploits earned him the nickname 'the Black Pimpernel', after the Scarlet Pimpernel – a character in a story set in the French Revolution.

FOREIGN SUPPORT

Using money that the ANC had built up over the years, Nelson was secretly taken out of South Africa to neighbouring Botswana and was then able to fly to many countries, including, Tanganyika, Ghana, Liberia and Ethiopia. In Algeria he underwent military training. Nelson also formed personal friendships with many African leaders on this trip.

'I will not leave South Africa, nor will I surrender. Only through hardship, sacrifice and **militant** action can freedom be won. The struggle is my life. I will continue fighting for freedom until the end of my days.'

Nelson Mandela, 26 June 1961, in a letter released to newspapers while he was on the run

THE RIVONIA TRIAL

While Nelson was in the west-African nation of Sierra Leone in December 1960 he received the news that Chief Luthuli of the ANC had been awarded the Nobel Peace Prize. The South African government, however, was angry that an ANC leader was so honoured. Soon Nelson was summoned back by the ANC and flown to a secret location in South Africa.

BEHIND BARS

Nelson went to the unofficial ANC headquarters at Lilliesleaf Farm in Rivonia, a rural suburb of Johannesburg. Nelson then travelled around South Africa checking on ANC units and their plans for action. Then, on the night of 5 August 1962, he was captured by police who had followed his trail.

Chief Albert Luthuli was awarded the Nobel Peace Prize only nine months after the Sharpeville tragedy.

Nelson's wife Winnie, his mother and other relatives attended the Rivonia trial in 1963.

Charged with leaving the country illegally, Nelson was convicted and sentenced to five years in prison.

THE BIG ARREST

Nelson was already in prison when South African police discovered the ANC military high command at Lilliesleaf Farm. Among the documents that they found was a plan called Operation Mayibuye, which outlined strategy for **guerrilla** warfare in South Africa. This news was political dynamite, and in October Nelson and ten other **activists** – including Walter Sisulu – were charged with **sabotage**.

The trial, which soon became known as the Rivonia Trial, began in October 1963. Nelson, Walter and the other defendants pleaded 'not guilty' to the charges on the grounds that the state (government) was not based on **democratic** ideals. South Africa – and the rest of the world – waited to see how the trial would develop. A verdict of guilty could lead to the death penalty.

LIFE IN PRISON

The state continued its case until 29 February 1964. The team of lawyers representing the **defendants** disagreed on whether the eleven should **testify**. Most of the defendants wanted to testify, partly to show that their plans for **sabotage** were not aimed at injuring people. In the end, they decided to make their statements.

Nelson spoke first, painting a picture of the inequality in South African life and how the ANC plans were not to promote **civil war** but to prepare for it. Walter Sisulu and the others continued this theme. Meanwhile, people held **vigils** in London and elsewhere in support of the defendants. The trial continued for months until eventually, on 11 June 1964, Nelson and the other main defendants were found guilty. They had to spend the night in suspense, waiting to see if they would be condemned to death.

THE ISLAND

On 12 June Nelson and the others were sentenced to life imprisonment. Nelson's wife Winnie and his mother were both in the courtroom but in the confusion Nelson never saw the look of relief on their faces. The news was indeed a relief, but Nelson and the other convicted men had to face an immense challenge – keeping their courage and even their **sanity** in a prison system that was even harsher to blacks than the rest of South Africans.

As if to prove this point, the state sent the prisoners to the **notorious** Robben Island prison, which stands several miles off Cape Town in Table Bay. A plane took the prisoners to the island, and when the seven convicts got off they were met by grim guards with automatic weapons. A cold winter wind blew off the sea, piercing the thin prison clothes. The guards did not speak to the prisoners except to utter one-word commands such as 'Halt', 'Move' or 'Silence'. It became clear immediately what 'life imprisonment' was to mean.

The notorious prison on Robben Island.

STERN DISCIPLINE

The hard lessons in discipline that Nelson had learned during his schooling worked to his advantage. Conditions were hard and the prisoners were forced to work long hours, either sewing clothes or crushing stones into gravel. The prison authorities allowed few visits from the prisoners' wives and families and made it almost impossible for them to find out what was happening in the outside world. Nelson could not be with his family to watch them grow, nor could he share in their grief when his eldest son died in a car crash in 1969.

Nelson Mandela and Walter Sisulu kept up their close friendship during their years in prison.

In order to boost **morale** and discipline, Nelson and many other prisoners read whatever books they could find. Some prisoners even studied for degrees while behind bars, and Robben Island was almost fondly known as 'the University' by those imprisoned there. Prisoners also learned a great deal from each other, and they formed circles to meet and discuss ideas.

Nelson also found that he was continuing his legal practice, even though it was in an unusual setting. Many prisoners were trying to form **appeals** against their convictions, but they lacked the legal knowledge to do this or the money to hire lawyers. Nelson offered his services to help prepare the necessary documents.

Nelson Mandela's words at the end of his trial in 1964 stand as one of the most dramatic statements of political ideals:
'I have fought against white domination and I have fought against black domination. I have cherished the ideal of a democratic and free society in which all persons live together in harmony and with equal opportunities. It is an ideal which I hope to live for and to achieve. But if needs be, it is an ideal for which I am prepared to die.'

DEALING WITH
THE ENEMY

L ife on Robben Island was **monotonous** and dreary despite the efforts that prisoners made to keep each other active, educated and cheerful. In many ways the worst part of prison life was not being able to help loved ones outside. Nelson's wife Winnie, who had become a leading activist, had a series of **banning orders** imposed on her and the police keep a watchful eye on all her activities. In 1975 Nelson saw his fifteen-year-old daughter Zindzi for the first time in twelve years. The meeting was emotional, made worse by a sad piece of news. Bram Fischer, one of the defence lawyers in the Rivonia Trial, had died of cancer. Fischer had been born into a privileged **Afrikaner** family but had devoted his life to helping the deprived majority within his country.

IGNORING THE BAIT

During these long years of imprisonment, Nelson came to learn that his reputation as a symbol of the African struggle had actually grown. The government also realized this and decided to tempt Nelson into making some **compromises**. They saw that Nelson's **opposition** to the **Bantustan** policy was an important stumbling block. In 1976 Nelson was visited by Jimmy Kruger, the South African Minister of Prisons. Kruger offered Nelson the chance to leave prison as long as he 'retired' to Transkei, which was one of the government's separate **homelands** for blacks. Nelson refused immediately.

SERIOUS BUSINESS

By 1980 there was a powerful 'Free Mandela' campaign launched in South Africa, which attracted widespread support around the world. There were also international sporting and cultural **boycotts** of South Africa because of its **apartheid** policies. The South African government felt threatened from all sides and put more pressure on Nelson to agree terms. In 1985 Kobie Coetsee, the Minister of Justice and one of the most important politicians in South Africa, visited Nelson.

Huge concerts and rallies, like this one in London, kept the 'Free Mandela' campaign in the international news.

The two men had a series of informal discussions and even became somewhat friendly with each other. Nelson remained firm that blacks and whites should not be separated in South Africa, and he insisted that the ANC might still need to use violence if the government did not make changes. Despite these unchanging views, he was willing to listen to Coetsee.

'South Africa belongs to all who live in it, black and white. We do not want to drive you into the sea.'
Nelson Mandela, addressing South African government officials in 1988

THE TASTE OF FREEDOM

One of Nelson Mandela's most consistent statements in all his discussions with South African government officials was simple: prisoners cannot enter into contracts. Only free men can **negotiate**. If one man was really the prisoner of the other, then any deal would be meaningless. Other events put pressure on the government. Many foreign companies were leaving South Africa because of **apartheid** and because of the violence that they feared could soon erupt there. The campaign to release Mandela was very popular among many white South Africans, and blacks had become impatient for change. By 1988 Nelson learned that none other than President P W Botha was planning to meet him.

TOP-LEVEL TALKS

Plans for this meeting were disrupted when President Botha suffered a **stroke** in January 1989. He resigned from active government but retained his position as **head of state**. In this role he still wanted to meet Nelson Mandela. The meeting between Nelson and the man known as 'die Groot Krokodil' ('the great crocodile') because of his stubborn temper finally took place on 5 July 1989. Although the meeting had a friendly tone, Botha refused Nelson's most important demand – to release all **political prisoners**. In August 1989 F W de Klerk became the new President of South Africa. Two months later he released Walter Sisulu and seven other famous Robben Island prisoners. They were not given **banning orders** and were allowed to speak legally as ANC representatives. The new president continued to make improvements by removing many of the restrictions imposed by apartheid. Nelson felt that de Klerk seriously wanted change and met him on 13 December 1989. Nelson pointed out that even if he were released, he and other ANC leaders making public speeches would have to be rearrested immediately if the ANC remained an illegal organization.

President PW Botha, 'the great crocodile'.

FREE AT LAST

It turned out that President de Klerk had listened to much of what Nelson had said. On 2 February 1990 he addressed the South African Parliament and made several dramatic announcements. He was to lift the bans on the ANC and 33 other organizations. He would free all political prisoners who were not convicted of violence and he would end **capital punishment**. 'The time for negotiation has arrived', he said.

Nelson Mandela, with his fist raised, walks out of prison on 11 February 1990.

A week later de Klerk invited Nelson to his office and informed him that he would be freed the next day. There was a short debate because, strangely enough, Nelson felt that the next day was too soon. He needed time to prepare for his release, and another week or so in prison would hardly count compared to all the years he had spent there. De Klerk, however, pointed out that foreign journalists had been told of the date and that he could not let them down. Nelson finally agreed, and the two men raised their glasses in a toast.

Nelson had been transferred from Robben Island to another prison in 1984, and spent his last five years in a more comfortable prison in Paarl, near Cape Town. It was through these prison gates that he walked, accompanied by his wife Winnie, on the afternoon of 11 February 1990. His 10,000 days in prison were over and at the age of 71 he was preparing to start a new life.

THE NEW SOUTH AFRICA

Most people in South Africa were ecstatic about Nelson Mandela's release. Crowds filled cities and towns in celebration. Cameras followed his every move as he greeted well-wishers at the prison gate and then from the window of a car as he was driven away. The first great reception, a Grand Parade by the city hall of Cape Town, set the tone for many similar expressions of joy and hope in South Africa.

However, Nelson never lost track of his role as a leader. Addressing an emotional gathering of 120,000 people in Soweto he promised to continue the struggle but also insisted that all South Africans unite to fight crime in the **townships**. In other speeches he praised the work of de Klerk and he persuaded the ANC to abandon the threat of violence as an act of **reconciliation**.

On 5 July 1990 Nelson Mandela was elected president of the ANC. In the next few years he used this role to press for more co-operation among all South Africans. His words were echoed by President de Klerk, who announced that general elections would be held in 1994.

'I am disturbed as many other South Africans no doubt are, by the **spectre** of a South Africa split into two hostile camps – blacks on one side...and whites on the other, slaughtering one another.'

Nelson Mandela in a memo to President P W Botha,
January 1989

PRESIDENT MANDELA

South Africa's general election in April 1994 was the first in which people of all races could vote. Nelson Mandela led the ANC to victory enabling the party to win 252 of the 400 seats in the South African Parliament. Near the end of the campaign Mandela debated F W de Klerk on television. At the end of the debate, which at times was heated, Mandela reached across to shake de Klerk's hand. He told his political opponent that 'I am proud to hold your hand for us to go forward.'

After becoming president in May 1994 Nelson Mandela tried to strengthen the ties between South

Nelson Mandela proudly – and publicly – casts his vote in his country's first free general election in 1994.

Africans instead of promoting the interests of just one racial group or political party. He helped draft a new South African **constitution**, which took effect in December 1996 and which guarantees basic rights to all citizens. At the same time the president approved new laws to improve the quality of health, housing and education for needy South Africans.

HEAD OF STATE

As president, Nelson Mandela became South Africa's head of state and a symbol of his country both at home and abroad. He represented the whole nation whether in delivering a New Year's Message to South Africa's Parliament or in laying the first brick for a new school in Soweto.

A visit by Nelson Mandela to a foreign city attracted thousands of well-wishers. These people were cheering not only for the courage and dignity of Mandela the man but also for the ideals of the new country that he had done so much to shape.

HEALING THE WOUNDS

Just as important, Mandela tried to change attitudes and to begin a time of healing in his country. One of the most significant moves was to establish the Truth and **Reconciliation** Commission. This group has heard the **testimony** of those who suffered injustices under the **apartheid** system and it has offered an **amnesty** for those prepared to appear before it. These people have included many – such as former police officers, soldiers and government officials – who had once kept apartheid in force.

INTERNAL PROBLEMS

The job of governing South Africa is not an easy one, and Nelson Mandela faced many difficulties from the start. One of his most important concerns was to make sure that the white population did not flee the country, in fear that the black **majority** would mount revenge attacks for all the past events under apartheid. Nelson included people of all races in his **cabinet**, and went to great lengths to show that South Africa is –

Archbishop Desmond Tutu, Chairman of the Truth and Reconciliation Commission, shakes hands with former South African president FW de Klerk.

and should remain – the mother country to all who live there. Nelson Mandela and F W de Klerk had shared the 1993 Nobel Peace Prize, and as president, Nelson Mandela tried to enlist the support of de Klerk in many political moves. The idea of these two men – from such different backgrounds – was a symbol of the moves to unite all South Africans.

Young black children arrive in 1996 for their first day at a previously all-white primary school.

There was another problem, this time from other black groups. The Zulu people, who represent a large proportion of the South African population, had long believed that their territory did not have enough **autonomy** to look after its own affairs. They continued to make this complaint after the 1994 election and their main political party, the Inkatha Freedom Party, even abandoned their seats in Parliament because of these disagreements.

CONTINUING VIOLENCE

It was not surprising that one of the first issues that Nelson Mandela addressed soon after his release was the problem of violence. Crime has always been a concern in the country, and it did not disappear overnight when free elections were held. Under President Mandela the South African police force had to change its character: instead of enforcing **apartheid** it had to concentrate on crime. The majority in the country can now respect the police, but violence remains a concern for all South Africans.

The memory of those who died and the prospect of more violence troubled Nelson Mandela during the time he was president.

The role of sport

South Africa is a sporting nation and most citizens follow their national teams, nicknamed the Springboks, with great enthusiasm. During the years of apartheid there was a sporting **boycott** of South Africa; the international community believed that this would put more pressure on the government to change conditions. The boycott was lifted after the 1994 election, so South African teams and individuals could compete around the world. South Africa hosted the 1995 World Cup for rugby – a sport usually associated with the **Afrikaner** population in South Africa. The Springboks won the World Cup, but their greatest joy was seeing President Mandela sharing in the celebrations at the stadium.

PASSING ON THE TORCH

Nelson Mandela turned 80 years old in July 1998. It was a time for reflection, and he announced that he would be stepping down as president when his term of office ended in 1999. He knew that he was too old to tackle the difficult day-to-day responsibilities of government. He also remembered how he, along with Walter Sisulu, Oliver Tambo and other young ANC members, had been impatient with the 'old' ANC leadership some 50 years before.

Nelson was pleased when the ANC chose a bright, younger politician, Thabo Mbeki, to replace him as ANC leader. Nelson had become a political 'father figure' to Mbeki, who had seen first-hand how the government operates. Nelson gave his full support to the ANC, and Mbeki, in the 1999 elections. The ANC won these elections easily and in an emotional moment in May 1999, Nelson stood down as president and made way for Thabo Mbeki.

Nelson Mandela was the first to congratulate Thabo Mbeki when he became South Africa's president in May 1999.

MANDELA THE MAN

Nelson Mandela and his wife, Graça Machel, are still very much in the public eye.

Nelson Mandela has had to make many sacrifices in his long life. One of the most painful aspects of his being a public figure – and in particular, one who has spent his time either on the run or in prison – is being separated from his family. In some ways, Nelson had an early introduction to such separations with the death of his father and his move to live with the **regent** as a child.

THE MARRIAGE COST

Nelson Mandela was still in his mid-twenties when he married Evelyn Mase, a cousin of Walter Sisulu. The couple had four children – two boys and two girls – although one of their daughters died as a child. They struggled to make ends meet but by the time Nelson had begun his own legal practice they had begun to grow apart. Evelyn grew increasingly religious and came to believe that the ANC was against religion. Nelson, for his part, believed that Evelyn's religious devotion made her more willing to accept the injustices of **apartheid**. The two finally divorced in 1956.

Nelson married Winnie Madikizela two years later. Winnie was a great support for Nelson and agreed with his aims within the ANC. Her house in Soweto became a centre for ANC activists while Nelson was serving his long prison sentence. However, in the late 1980s Winnie became associated with rough young men who tortured – and in one case, killed – other black people who did not agree with them. Nelson could not support her involvement and they, too, were divorced.

Nelson Mandela, addressing the General Assembly of the United Nations, receives a standing ovation.

Having been released from prison, Nelson Mandela became friendly with Graça Machel, the widow of the great Mozambique freedom fighter Samora Machel. The two were married in 1998 and became a popular couple within South Africa.

In 1995 Nelson Mandela returned to visit Robben Island and paused to hammer stones in the same yard where he had done hard labour 30 years before.

THE INTERNATIONAL ARENA

Almost as soon as Nelson Mandela was released from prison he was swamped with invitations to address various groups across the globe. He has received honorary degrees from more than 50 international universities and colleges. On an official level he visited many countries and met with political leaders. One of his most famous trips was to the United States in 1990. While there he received a medal from the US Congress in Washington and addressed the United Nations in New York City. Typically, while in New York, he made a point of attending a rally in the deprived area of Harlem, where many black Americans still live in poverty. When Nelson Mandela received the 1993 Nobel Peace Prize (with F W de Klerk) he dedicated the prize to all who worked for peace and stood against racism.

THE BIRTHDAY BASHES

It is at home in South Africa where Nelson Mandela's message has had its greatest effect. Despite continuing difficulties in the country, South Africans mark each Mandela birthday (18 July) with parties. Nelson invited 1000 disabled children to his 79th birthday

Simple tastes

Perhaps the best reflection of Nelson Mandela's personal side is his daily routine. His strict sense of self-discipline continues to dictate his actions in the same way that it did while he was serving his sentence on Robben Island and other prisons. He still wakes up at 4.30 am no matter how late he has worked the previous evening. By 5 am he has begun an exercising routine that lasts for at least an hour. At 6.30 am he has a breakfast of plain porridge, fresh fruit and milk, while reading the newspapers, and then works at least twelve hours. He drinks little alcohol apart from the occasional glass of sweet white wine.

party in 1997 and the welcome he gave them was as genuine as the welcome he gave the world leaders who celebrated his eightieth birthday.

In 1998, when Nelson Mandela turned 80, South Africa organized a series of concerts entitled 'Gift to the Nation'. These marked the launch of a year-long series of celebrations honouring Mandela, right through to his retirement as president. Party-goers were amused and cheered by the sight of their elderly president singing and clapping along with rap musicians, rock bands and symphony orchestras, as well as a range of traditional African musical groups.

As the century draws to a close, Nelson Mandela now lives in Qunu, his childhood village. So much happened while he was away – and he can reflect on the fact that he was responsible for many of those changes.

NELSON MANDELA – TIMELINE

1918	(18 July) (Nelson) Rolihlahla Mandela born in the Transkei village of Mvezo
1934	Attends Clarkebury Boarding Institute
1937	Enrols at Healdtown, a **missionary** college
1938–40	Attends University College of Fort Hare
1941	Completes degree course by **correspondence** at University of South Africa
1942	Joins African National Congress (ANC)
1944	Becomes co-founder of African National Congress Youth League (ANCYL)
1946	Marries Evelyn Mase
1947	Elected to the **Secretaryship** of the ANCYL
1949	Promotes the Programme of Action at ANC national conference
1950	Elected to the National Executive Council (NEC) of the ANC
1952	Elected National Volunteer-in-Chief of the ANC's Campaign for the Defiance of Unjust Laws
1952	Cleared of charges of **inciting** violence
1952	Elected to the presidency of ANCYL and becomes a deputy president of the ANC itself
1952	Opens law practice in Johannesburg with his friend Oliver Tambo as partner
1956	Divorces Evelyn
1957	Charged with **treason** but found not guilty
1958	Marries Winnie Madikizela
1961	Becomes Commander-in-Chief of Umkhonto we Sizwe, the armed branch of the ANC
1962	Leaves South Africa secretly to tour other African nations and to gain support and military training for the ANC
1962	Arrested on his return to South Africa for having left the country illegally Convicted and sentenced to five years' imprisonment

1963	Charged with **sabotage** while in prison after the secret ANC headquarters are discovered
	Faces possible death sentence if convicted
1964	Rivonia Trial ends with a conviction; sentence is life imprisonment
	Sent to Robben Island Prison near Cape Town
1976	Meets Jimmy Kruger, South Africa's Minister for Prisons but refuses to trade freedom for recognition of **homelands**
1985	Meets Kobie Coetsee, Minister of Justice
	No agreement, but preparation for future high-level meetings
1989	Meets President P W Botha but fails to reach agreement on terms for a release from prison
1989	Meets new President, F W de Klerk, and comes to terms for release
1990	(11 February) released from prison
1990	(5 July) elected President of the ANC
1993	Awarded (with F W de Klerk) the Nobel Peace Prize
1994	Elected South Africa's president in country's first election where all South Africans can vote
1998	Divorces Winnie Mandela and marries Graça Machel
1999	Retires from active politics at the end of his five-year term as president

GLOSSARY

activist someone who devotes time and energy to a cause

Afrikaner white South African whose ancestors came from the Netherlands

aggressive actively against something, sometimes threatening violence

amnesty official pardon

ancestors people in the past who were part of the same family or group

apartheid system of government rules that made whites and blacks live apart from each other in South Africa

appeal a legal case aimed at reversing the outcome of a previous case

articled clerk someone who is training to be a lawyer and is gaining work experience in a law firm

autonomy freedom for an area to look after its own business, with little involvement by the country's government

BA degree Bachelor of Arts degree – a certificate that shows someone has passed a higher-level course of study

banning orders government documents that limit where someone can go as well as what they can do

Bantustan government policy of moving black people to several areas within South Africa to remove them from white-only areas

boycott to avoid dealing with a company, service or even a country in order to force them to change

cabinet closest advisors to a political leader, who help govern a country

capital punishment death sentence in criminal cases

chauffeur someone who is paid to drive others in a private car

chronicle to relate the history of someone or something such as a nation

civil disobedience protesting against unfair laws by legal means such as marches and demonstrations

civil war war between two or more groups within a country

clan group of related families

colonial refers to countries that are being ruled by other countries

coloureds (in South Africa) people of mixed white and black background

communist a supporter of a system of government in which property and industry are controlled by the government, and not by individuals

compromise agreement where two sides each give in a little

conservative cautious and unwilling to change things in politics

constitution written document that dictates how a country or organisation will be run as well as stating its aims

correspondence course course where you study by post

counsel to provide advice to someone

defendant someone who is accused of a crime in court

democratic refers to democracy, or the right of all people in a country to have an equal chance in life

elders older members of a tribe or other social group

establishment collectively, the people who own, rule or write about a country

ethnic having to do with people's nationality or race

expelled forced to leave

founding official start of an organization

grassroots basic level, as in the widest level of support for a cause

groomed prepared for some

responsibility

guardian someone with the legal right to act as someone else's parent

guerrilla small-scale warfare, often involving hiding in the countryside to fight larger armies

head of state someone who acts as a symbol of a country

homelands places where black South Africans had to live under apartheid

honorary degree award given by a university or college to someone who is well respected

incite to persuade people to do something, such as taking action against a government

magistrate government official who acts as a judge in local matters

majority greater part of something

militant supporting, or a supporter of, violent action in order to achieve political aims

minority smaller part of something

missionary promoting a religious view, usually Christian

monotonous boring and unchanging

morale sense of confidence and shared views within an organisation

negotiations peaceful discussions to solve a dispute

notorious famous in a bad way

opposition strongly-held view against something

parliamentary representation right to elect people to represent a group

petitions letters signed by many people asking a government for something

political prisoner a prisoner whose crime was committed because of a disagreement with the government of a country

prejudice unwillingness to accept that all people are equal

preside to have control over a group

racism belief that the lives of some people, such as white people or blacks, are not as important as those of other people

radical favouring extreme solutions to a problem

reconciliation bringing together of opposing groups

regent someone who acts in place of a king or prince

sabotage deliberate destruction of things for a political reason

safe house an address where someone can hide, in order to escape capture by the police

sanity ability to think clearly

secretaryship ruling group of an organisation

spectre ghostly symbol

State of Emergency time when many rights, such as free speech, are withdrawn because a government fears violence

stroke sudden illness due to blockage in the blood supply to the brain

suspended sentence criminal sentence that is spent away from prison but under observation

taunting making fun of in a very public way

testify to make a statement in court

testimony actual statement when someone testifies

township local area, like a town or city, where blacks had to live under apartheid

treason crime of trying to overthrow the government

underground in secret, and usually hiding from the police and other powers

vigil long period of time that people spend together to show support for someone or something

warrant document that is used in a court of law

INDEX